K N O T

Poems by Forrest Gander

Photographs by Jack Shear

MW EDITIONS

COPPER CANYON PRESS

O time, thou must untangle this, not I,
It is too hard a knot for me t'untie.

Twelfth Night (2.2.40–41)

Exhausted. I can't climb anymore. Yet I could, possibly, hang here for a moment, stop this exertion, just cling, catching my breath, to this cascade of long dark hair which she has let down from the window. The window that didn't look nearly so high, only balcony level, wasn't it? when I started. Those hours ago. Haven't I been climbing for hours? Above me, my overextended arms quiver and ache all the way down to their sockets; the round swollen muscles of my shoulders press to my ears. Is she calling? I can't hear. When I look up, I see the cascade of her long hair, nothing beyond that. But it's as difficult to pause as to climb, so I keep going. To tell the truth, I never paused. Deaf and blind, I keep tugging myself up into that falling blackness. I who am bringing her the moon.

As long as I hold this up, you cannot see me, you don't know who or what I am or why the cloth's weave has no luster, no pilling, no shading. I am almost invisible. And when finally my hand trails the rest of me inside, where only enough room remains, exactly enough room, for that single hand, the one still lifted above my head holding the cloth, the *I* which used to be *me* will have disappeared completely, and the material will no doubt tumble to the floor as though there never were anything inside it, nothing filling it out. Or just a capricious spirit. Or just a fleet intimation of form. What was that, anyway? Don't tell me it was a life. Just my wrist, my thumb, my curled fingers. They constitute all that remains. A green glow at the ocean's horizon after the sun has gone down. Something like that. Already not even something, really, only a particle of something attached to what merely seemed substantial but was, instead, the nothing. To which I am subject. To which I granted so much scope that it crowded me out and I became my own ghost. But inside the darkness. Inside the. In.

I am not ashamed. It's not in shame that I walk toward you with my face and genitals covered. The cloth doesn't shield me so much as it shields you. I am too beautiful. Simply too beautiful. The scored striations in my thighs, the marvelous balls of my feet, the flutes of my clavicles, how could you begin to see them? You've never come across anything so gracefully sheathed inside itself. I inhabit all my body at once, to the fullest extent, every cell brimming. The particles of air I displace as I walk toward you convene in my wake to gossip over the shapeliness they so briefly caressed. Behind me there is always that whispering. Look, even my shadow tries to resemble me. The throbbing vein in my throat has no likeness, and if my sex didn't remain a secret—there is simply no telling. I cover myself as a mercy, believe me. Because you have no idea about this kind of beauty. Behold me and you would know you've lived your life in a closed coffin. Are you ready for that? I take another step toward you and darkness streams over me, darkness flocks, it affixes to me like a shroud, a bruise. For so many have bruised themselves to be near me.

What are you holding so tightly?
     You can see it's a corpse.
But where are you taking it?
     It goes where I go.
Aren't you far ahead of the funeral procession?
     It's a private affair.
Meaning it's someone you loved?
     Someone I would have loved to see
     make better choices.
In time, things will get better for you.
     You don't know that. What's
     to come is just
     the sentence of my duration.
You don't think feelings can change?
     If time were some sort of measurement
     of change, it stopped for me.
Say what you will, don't you still have the present
and your own choices to make?
     You think that between the past and the future
     there's an interval in which I'm
     considering your question. But there is no interval.
You don't believe in the present?
     My future is what I carry my corpse into.

Then I heard a voice say, *You have made of your burden a house and you have become trapped in that house. All its spacious rooms have solidified and incarcerated you there. But when you understand what you have done, you will find you can lift your house upon your shoulders, and it will be light enough to carry with you.*

I have no faith in disembodied voices, I thought. And indeed, when I lifted the house to my shoulders, I found it grievously heavy. The only way to hold so much weight, I realized as my muscles began to give out, was by stripping the house of its associative meanings, all its windows and doors, sucking up its interior, compressing its many rooms into one room. I needed to minimize the separation between house and body.

Even so, I continued to feel the extreme downwardness of its weight, and my head collided constantly with the ceiling and walls. Nor could I step out from beneath the darkness that now surrounded me. It became clear that rather than accepting the house for what it had become, a limiting container, I would have to reestablish our relation in fresh terms. I would need to go further into the house, to align my coordinates with its own so that we might be, finally, a collaborative function with no volume, no color, no openings, no inside or outside. A totality. A mourning. It was my understanding that lifted the house.

Well done, I heard the voice say again. *But at this point it would be wrong to put down the house, for you have become its foundation. This is the charge of your understanding.*

You who suppose you cannot carry what you've incurred, look at me. Like the component species of a lichen, I gave something up to become something else. And I am impenetrable, inviolable, without the dimension necessary for anything to breach me. If I manifest a deficiency of being in relation to being itself, at least my lock can't be picked.

This evening I heard someone ask, *What's that?* And someone else answer, *That's nothing, just a house running away on two legs.*

But every person's word shall be their burden.

Who can know if there's a world beyond what you see until I happen?

I who am more than some man with his retinue of black river. I have everything to do with you.

But the transposition of myself into this undulating, fluvial gesture in which dream becomes thought, in which desire becomes being, is no anarchic moment.

Would you like a little advice? Don't be so afraid of the silence. It isn't abyss, it's the fullness, the beyond-ache.

At last you've recognized me, the angel of history stepping backward into the future while the past spools out and flutters away in front of me, the compulsive restlessness of its flurry forming a grammar— Listen now,

it is speaking of you. Can you hear? Have you gone incognito again?

Ah, you're distracted by the licorice smell of freshly mowed anise. A tree blazing green with fireflies.

All the while I'm here, just a little up-trauma from you in black and white,

stumbling blindly back into the infinite depth that excludes you from its next moment.

And there is no plan, no goal, least of all your heroization. What was it, anyway, you thought made you so special?

Did you fantasize that your initials were tattooed on my nates? Sorry to break it to you, but your every aspiration was microscopic.

And besides, weren't you forever looking in the wrong direction, which is to say inward? So you missed the other signs, the other roads, and now your onward has run out.

And still, you would reach for my hand?

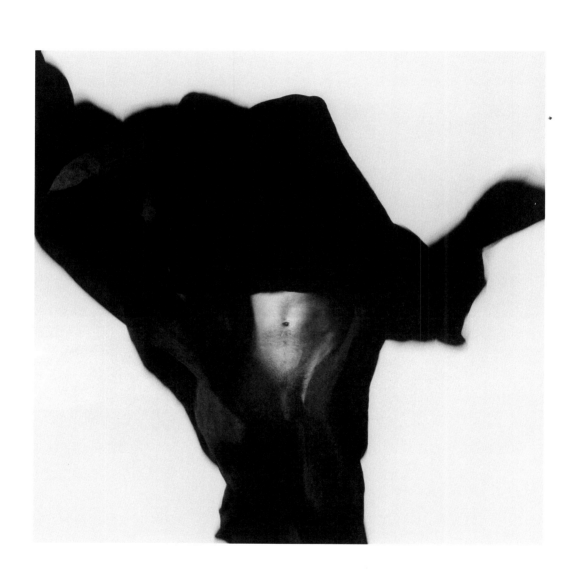

You tear open the packaging to reveal this gallery

of myself still wrapped in the felt. And there

you have it: a window to the soul.

Such an elegance of casual

simplicity. Doesn't the coat of arms

of every heraldry celebrate

my own escutcheon? It's said,

the sentence of my gender

is written with a dangling

modifier. And if you look

closely, you'll make out

a suspensory ligament

anchoring the ringed clapper,

a confluence of twilit tributaries

flooding the pelvic inlet. Still, I'm

hidden as a celebrity. And would you like it

better if I were more exposed? If you

could trace with finger or tongue

the bilateral angulation of hair

flowing inward from my thighs? Not

even your birthday—and already the surprise.

Say what? What did you say?

    That when I stepped from the mouth of the labyrinth

    into the arena, I was embarrassed by all the roaring—

    as though I were some revelation

    you'd longed for, if only you could

    remember of what.

I can't hear with all that

howling and screaming. Who did you say you were?

    A stillness with a destination. Which is your eyes.

But what are you waiting for?

    I wanted to learn if I could be saved

    by anyone's intervention. But you are shitless scared.

Why does your attendant just stand there

watching you watch us?

    Under the cloth, my muscles tense and relax, pulsing.

But who are you really?

    Forget the physical difference between us

    and you'll know for sure.

Is that some kind of riddle?

    In the density of my shape you'll see what's been exorcised

    from the bitterness and self-disappointment at your core.

Remember when there was world and you, with that leopardine snarl in your eyes, were one of its lords? You really didn't expect the horizon to blur and fade like an expiration date. Not in your lifetime. Or for the multitudes to choke out so quickly. But by then, your self-loathing didn't leave much room for others. So the oceans belched, and tiny particles of ash fell over everything like the dandruff of some despotic god.

Here, just sitting here, I gather my strength, subject to the filtered shadow that stipples my skin. Each day sticks its thin tubes of light through my veil, intubating me. From morning to afternoon, something slowly crawls across the roof of my tent like a tarantula. Now and then, I feel faint traces of breeze.

But I have endless patience. My gestation takes place in the subjunctive, the yet-to-be. Peer in and you can imagine the preexpression on my face.

Unsupervised, I listen intently for reports from your world. The reports sound a lot like weeping. At night, when I can see absolutely nothing, I focus on the ticking of cockroaches across the sprung bamboo floor. An effervescence of tiny detonations in my good ear.

I could be a seed. Sown here.

Or some kind of child with receding gums and a widow's peak.

My time comes after, when at last I'm allowed to enter your story. Until then, dormancy is my occupation. Shuttered against you, I await my conscription.

If I touch myself, and I do, my skin feels vague and remote, like Naugahyde. Pins and needles in my feet, a kind of discharge from one eye. My asshole itches. With my good ear, I hear things yet to take place. Like your confession, which has yet to take place. My one hand clenches the other.

In all your strategies, in your see-through dreams, I'm only a smudge of becoming. Did you think you would solve me? But each wave of your observance buckles into a loosening sureness.

Were rivers really riven once with fish? Were there other birds than just these? Now a genius-system disseminates the idea of crow into the few remaining trees, and the stimulation of your senses gets measured out in installments.

Somewhere in the theater of my mind, a flowerpecker twitters behind a palm leaf. The moon leaves its corrugated imprint on rippling water.

And you? Can you even remember the high points, how you once plunged into your love steadily, slowly, searchingly, like the beam of a lighthouse? These days your regrets hive in you like worms in a cadaver. Is that why you keep glancing in my direction?

Now is nothing. Look at the days you've wasted. I am yet to come.

And then I catch myself   vanishing into the mouth of

                                        my own deformed shadow

        which has peeled up   from the earth & glommed

    to my chest, my   face, suffocating me,

                        sucking me forward in   a grotesque pas de deux,

        into it, into   what

                                        now?

Minotaur: *So I ask again. Why can't you follow my directive?*

Prisoner: It's as though my mourning is all edged with some other day's light and what I think of as my presence goes blank when it wakes.

Minotaur: *My gesture embarrasses you, doesn't it? You're afraid it could bring you back to life?*

Prisoner: I'm worried that each interpretation leads me back to its shadings, into another night.

Minotaur: *Here, within my cloak, there is only dreaming. And what you're afraid you deserve remains hidden.*

Prisoner: Inside my own dark, a deeper darkness connives with the light.

Minotaur: *Because looking is immediate, it demands patience. But if you had that, you would have escaped me and I'd have sputtered out like a wick.*

Prisoner: The curse of my face, which you love. My likeness, you keep repeating, to no one else.

Only the eyes   of my knees see

where I'm going   as I haul, above   my fine-haired thighs,

some Rorschach blot,   some scrap of   another universe

devoid of starlight,   and aren't you just

as lost as me   though you fix your gaze   on that strip of my flesh

flashing   like the nakedness   beneath a dressing-room door   as you try to

coax   what's not there   into being—the

throne of my pelvis,   dangling cock, my   torso, throat, face, hair—

all absorbed into   this swirling nimbus   I wear.

When he came out, he was dressed I guess as a bat, waving

his arms under a huge cloth that completely swallowed his

head. No one paid him any mind at first,

and somebody changed the music and poured pisco

sours, and someone else lit a joint, but the guy didn't

stop moving his arms—very slowly—standing in front

of the fireplace kind of in the middle of things. We

couldn't see his face, and pretty soon we ran out of stuff

to say to each other and we sat there just watching him.

Who is that? the girl next to me whispered, but nobody

answered. The black wings slowly, rhythmically flapping

not as though to take flight but as though to tell us

something we sure as shit didn't want to know about.

In looking at me,   you contract me   to inhabit you, for I stand

here   as though I've washed up

from nowhere with no   context, no history, nothing   behind me and

only you, you before me   like a trembling bull   for whom I wave this

cape, and yet I occupy   no place but in your eyes and so you can

do to me and think of me   whatever you want

I'm a faceless lifetime of muscle-   memory fetched-up onto a stage

and if I disappear   I'll be gone   not only from sight but from

all experience   but your own, for I'm inside   you now, and   though you can't

remember everyone,   you can't forget me.

For hours you've been standing above the battlefield, your eyes fixed as though pinned in place
   by needles. What do you see down there?

   I see that plain of undifferentiated blackness flaring up to meet me.

Are you just thinking your answer? You haven't said a word all day.

   My voice has gone off to be by itself. Like an echo. There's a horrible low
      buzzing of sonic radioactivity in my brain.

Is it vengeance you want?

   It's Patroclus I want. This morning I kissed the inside of his sandal. I want the
      craving that enters my body when I breathe in the scent of his sweat.

Why are you just mumbling to yourself? What are you up to?

   His death has translated me. Look, there's an eel writhing under my shoulder
      and my eyes are stretched holes in leather. My new state doesn't fit well
         with life.

How can you go on just staring like that into his absence?

   This is my moment of— My last glance before total darkness. Listen: Have you
      ever sprayed a large spider with poison and seen it go insane, shriveling and
         clutching itself, screaming soundlessly, pulsing in a frenzy and then
            unballing its legs, still alive? I am that spider.

Did I just hear your heartbeat skip?

   I'm switching off the sky. Kiss me goodnight.

My body is   my own, but the rest

is the flux   of who I'll become.

Trauma makes me   what I am.

My eyes, even my

face, is loosened   by agitation because

I'm searching   for someone who

isn't you, who   isn't even

out there, where   you are.

It's true, I'm unmistakable

in this empty space, the   core of nothing, the

message   in a bottle, but   when you bow your head

to read me,   there is no

message. Just the intervallic cockroach-

scurry forward   of your own

ravenous appetite

for more.

As though an archive of the human body were spilling from a sack: here

is the biceps of an athlete, a sleek erotics jutting out from

 a burial plan. Did you think you had some right to

my gaze? I only asked for a glimpse

 of the future. Oblivion comes for all of us.

  My life entered & turned out the light.

Anything to be rid of you!   I fling away your ample shadow,

that cloud of human form,   but then I haul it in again

as though I'm working out   a debt I never expected

to incur. My bulging   buttocks: the bride-white

tension of a soap bubble.   Your urge to cling: a torrent

of swarthy need. We are two   distinct systems, incompatible,

though our separation is   pointless. Besides, look—I'm still

reaching out my hand.

I stripped off my clothes on the backseat of the bus and kicked out

the emergency door dragging this blanket full of lice after me I ran

right past the rusty pickup following the bus

the old farmer had his window down

and his radio was playing Ode to Joy *this is right where I want to be*

I said to myself as I lifted the blanket and it poured out around me

like sorghum from a split barrel they set the dogs after me of course

but my heart is a horse this is right where I want to be I noticed a

tiny whirlwind of dust keeping pace on the side of the road the smell

of coming rain I could hear dogs barking and I felt thirstier for

everything I wasn't slowing down I passed a street corner empty

except for one man leaning back into all those faded papers stapled

to the telephone pole he was wearing dark glasses playing a clarinet

he didn't even notice me I've got a voice like an ice pick and

I didn't say a word though I wanted to shout *hey look it's me*

I have inherited the earth and not a single shadow I will never be lonely but I

hadn't come to speak my mind I'd come to be spoken of

Tell me what you see.

      A man. A naked man.

What else?

      A black cloth. Quite large, folded over him.

And?

      The man seems to be diving upward

      through the cloth as through a wave.

      Twisting into it

      as it collapses over him.

Or?

      Yes. Or being spun out from it.

Where does your eye linger?

      At first the nipple

      peering out from his chest,

      but no. It's the shapely curve

      of the outer thigh from the knob

      of his hip to his knee. That muscle

      swelling outward and rhyming

      with the hang of the cloth. And

      wait, now I see! Everything else

      is a diversion.

When finally I let go of my self-pity, when
I sloughed off the garment of my grief,
hoisting it furiously over my head,
I discovered myself
wondering what would come next.
But it's you, isn't it?

You've caught me unsleeved. Washed
clean, a bud after rain. And it's clear
to you that my body isn't only the shaft
of an archaic instrument. It's a communion
you want to share. With my eyes covered,
of course you're free to take me in. But

wouldn't you like even more? Can
you sate yourself on just my vitality, my
pure form? I've already entered
your experience sensorially, not
as mere information. And however much you stare,
I stand beyond any place where your command,
your flirting, your feigned closeness reaches.
As the seen thing, I'm immutable and still
worth your attending to. And it could be
I'll let you go further if you give me a hand
lifting this last blindness from my face.

What do you see?

A divinity wrung from a black cloud.

Are you the kind who prefers your god without a body?

It's his nakedness that shields me from distraction.

But your eyes, they can't edge close enough, can they?

Like a cat fixed on a bird out of reach.

What is it you want?

I want only what I can't see: something other than myself.

But the divinity vanishes when you turn away, doesn't he?

Yes, but my stare has already left its spider-bite on his inner thigh.

What is it you really want?

You think I'm at liberty to say? I'm not.

The speech balloon
has gone missing, but still
the silence crackles. In a dark
seam of disturbance
you suck hard for any air
the fire hasn't eaten.
Your arms flap from your
vanishing point. Your
mind in the updraft,
smoke rises in your throat.
Kindness and daylight
will outlive you, but what
did you ever have to do
with either? You, who
poked the tunneling
larva of disappointment
into a hairline crack
in the heart of the one
who loved you most. You
can't be surprised, glancing
back over your shoulder now,
eyes wide, pupils
dilated, at the wake of
unmanageable pain, the
devastation. And because your words
carried so much weight,
the given length of your
time here
has snapped off prematurely.
Cauterized, thrust into this
torrent of heat,
you are
and are not.

POET'S NOTE

In 2018, the irrepressibly image-driven Jack Shear shared with me some digital photographs from what have come to be three distinct bodies of work. Like many artists, he is drawn to seriality. There were portraits of men with closed eyes, abstract architectural studies, and dynamic nudes and seminudes, in which the familiarly articulate lineaments of male musculature are partly hidden from us by a black linen cloth. But the cloth is so energized by its contact with the human body that it takes on a life of its own—and not just a life but a dimension. Body and cloth act out a provocative ballet, a wrestling match, a tense sequence of appearances and disappearances that immediately take on symbolic weight. What do we feel encountering these shifting, explosive dramas of primary elements, naked body and eclipse? I was mesmerized and asked to see more. They came: dreamy, violent, mythic, and elemental. For the last three years, I have carried them in my mind everywhere. When, in 2021, Jack sent me large prints of these images, I set them up around the room and knew I could write my way into them.

ABOUT THE POET

Forrest Gander is a writer and translator with degrees in geology and literature. Among his many books are *Be With*, winner of the 2019 Pulitzer Prize for Poetry, *Twice Alive: An Ecology of Intimacies*, and his novel *The Trace*. Gander's translations include *It Must Be a Misunderstanding* by Coral Bracho, *Spectacle & Pigsty* (winner of the Best Translated Book Award) by Kiwao Nomura (translated with Kyoko Yoshida), and *Then Come Back: The Lost Neruda Poems*, a collection of previously unpublished and untranslated poems by Pablo Neruda. He has been awarded grants from the Library of Congress, the Solomon R. Guggenheim Foundation, the George A. and Eliza Gardner Howard Foundation, the Whiting Foundation, and United States Artists. Gander was born in the Mojave Desert and lives in Northern California.

ABOUT THE ARTIST

Jack Shear is a photographer whose passion for the medium dates to his youth in Los Angeles. His work emphasizes portraiture and nudes and is represented in several permanent museum collections, including the San Francisco Museum of Modern Art and the Whitney Museum of American Art in New York City. His work has been exhibited in solo shows at the Yale School of Art in New Haven and Le Musée Territorial in Saint Barthelémy, among other venues. He has published two previous books, *Four Marines and Other Portraits* and *Short Season: Portrait of a Minor League Baseball Team*. In 2016, an exhibition and accompanying catalogue, *Borrowed Light: Selections from the Jack Shear Collection*, featured selections from a gift of over two thousand art-historical photographs he donated to the Tang Teaching Museum at Skidmore College in Saratoga Springs, New York. Shear lives and works in New York City and Spencertown, New York.